All that we can't leave behind

Carl Perry

BookLeaf Publishing

Presentation by *BookLeaf Publishing*

Web: www.bookleafpub.com

E-mail: info@bookleafpub.com

ISBN: 9789357213400

First edition 2023

Snow

You come in over
frostbitten snow
with eyes pleading,
whilst grasping on to
a soft blanket
and jacket to keep you warm.

You cant come in again,
know that when you leave
the door will be shut and
things cant be the same,
any footsteps left in the falling snow
wont be easily retraced.

Empty rooms

The creak of the door

spurs me further inside,

its slow whine

alerts the silence,

I fumble along walls

to the light switch,

click

and I am illuminated

amongst my surroundings.

I wander in footsteps

lightly on the floorboards

and peer into empty rooms,

I am alone here.

I turn and face

a reflection of a man

I haven't seen before.

Ghost

There's a ghost inside this house,
he lives in a little room
at the back,
out of the way.
Abiding by himself
even his thoughts are not his friends.
His mind is torn
between
his doubts,
his fears,
the great unknown
and the future.

He cannot shake it off,
though he floats around
as if in a day dream,
it seems the feeling
is there to stay,
eating him away
day after day.

Negative space

I occupy only

one third of a
three-seater sofa,
one chair at a
two seat dining table,
the lonely side of a double bed.

The rest is just
negative space
where I keep glancing
at seats collecting dust;
the hollowness of the shell
of a life I have built
inside four walls.

Outside life goes by,
the leaves turn
and cars leave.

Brush with cold

Late at night,

sometimes,

in my half-slept daze

I'll roll over

whilst trying to get comfortable

and my leg will brush

the cold emptiness

of the other side of my double bed.

The jolt to my skin

sends my eyes awake

and in the darkness

I face the room alone.

I sometimes fear

this brush with cold,

the lack of someone warm

beside me

is unsettling,

and before I go back to sleep

I will wish

for you to be there the next night.

Void

A second

seems to last an age

in this dead space.

An hour

never seems to come.

I've created my own

void,

and all time slows.

Day breaks, light glares,

rain splashes, winds tear,

night surrounds.

The colour of my life

feels grey,

and this feeling is lost on me.

I am only sunken,

trying to make sense of it.

The clocks hands still

turn,

but I am rooted in place.

Well

I sip the last of the beer

and take a walk,

leaving warmth,

into the night,

with blurry lights passing

the engines roar louder

then fade to quiet.

I fumble the phone out of my pocket,

press the lock button

for a sign.

Nothing.

I reach the door,

turn keys

and let it slam shut

as I blindly press the light.

In the dreary

stairwell I climb uneven steps.

Another door

is turned open and left to slam.

I pick out the phone,

hoping,

and press unlock.

Nothing,

wishing coins

in a darkened well.

as it moves to break

as it moves to break

you try

to swim with the tide,

picking up the pieces

whilst

dropping them at the

same time.

comfort is secondary

to the need and want

of them closer;

or just the sight of them.

it greets you and beats

you,

to within an inch of your

psychological limit

just before you scream

"I cant take it anymore".

and you call

(or text

depending on your

technological know-how)

and wait
hoping they answer your

wasted hearts plea.

but the next morning

realisation takes the

wheel.

# of waiting...

The lonely man sits

huddled up in the armchair,

just enough paces away

from the front door

to get there quick enough.

The coffee cup on the stand

is getting colder,

he doesn't notice.

The TV flickers

with the pressing of remote,

no change of mind.

Someone knocks...

he goes to the front door.

A trick of the senses.

He returns to the chair;

stares at the coffee table.

The picture is still the same;

the candle still burns.

Ache

It tightens

at the chest, (just beneath the ribcage)

until the swirling

vortex of thoughts

and crushing weight

betrays

the whole self.

This ache,

that bears down

over the years, (of longing)

an implant

on the mind,

an imprint

on the soul.

This ache,

it stays in wait

in the crux of every vein, (a permanence)

it does not escape

and the mark is felt

every passing day.

Loop

Reaching back

over the tall grass

he espied his undoing

floating amongst the fronds of

the bronze brown hair,

those bewitching eyes

suspended in animation.

The little irises of green

pierced underneath

digging deep

and relentlessly,

pushing aside the golden sun

ignoring the wisps of clouds

as they float along.

My mind replays the meeting,

inside this fictitious glade,

we're still the same

only the place has changed.

Our pupils meet

but it echoes and ripples

on a loop in my head

on a loop in my head

on a loop in my head

on a loop in my head…

Past lives

Young and hopeful we ran

through these streets

and alleyways

turning in and out through barriers

to the different houses and greens

laughing.

Now I walk these streets again,

years have passed,

the fences broken and falling

the trees overhang

and old passages built on,

only the concrete remains.

The houses where they once were

have changed,

the people left

and no youths run the streets.

The greens contain "no ball games" signs

and the playfulness is lost.

Maybe we're all lost now

or just older

seeking hope in new houses on new roads.

Only the concrete remains.

Creek

Beside the small flowing water

I watch, kneeling down,

as I drop a stone

into the clearness

and see it sink

to the rocks beneath

while ripples continue on top.

They ebb outwards

as the sun beats down,

I look along the bank

to the willow branch leaves

barely off the surface,

the wind sweeping them

from side to side.

I turn to see my friends,

climbing a tree

to reach the swing,

their youthful nonchalance

written in excitement

across their faces.

They take it in turns

to reach the other side

each leaping across the void.

I realise I am next.

I take the rope...

Meadow

Beyond the panes

of the varnished rain-sealed fence

lay a field,

a meadow

filled with green.

I'd first seen it

with my youthful eyes

while it was lit up

like a sea of metal

on the summer day.

We'd cracked and shifted

a panel of fence.

crept into the sea

and ran.

To ourselves this was the gateway

to the rest of the world.

We ran to the nearest

largest tree

and turned back...

we never got further.

Over trees

The winding parkway

skirts the city,

wind filling the space

in the beaten Land Rover.

I look across

over houses and trees

to the gleaming white stands

of London Road,

floodlights looming even higher.

I am taken back

in those seconds of the glance

to childhood,

and youthful days

spent watching football,

decked out in full kit.

A coca-cola at half time

and a bag of crisps

with my friend and his dad.

We cheer as our team loses,

then go home

to the patch of grass outside

where we re-enact our own match.

Empty field

Onto coloured swings
rusted metal chains
and tall grass
the distant winter sun
settles its light on climbing frames,
unused.

Where have they gone?
The kids of yesterday
those who were unafraid:
of letting go when the swing reached
the highest point,
of scraped knees
and hands covered in bark.

They are not here,
gone to play inside
and while away the time
couch surfing
and playing video games 'til late,
misspent hours of the lost youth.

Onto coloured swings
and worn down climbing frames,
the sun lights up
that empty field.

Photoframe

If only there was
a forgotten hallway,
empty of other souls,
with pictures
hanging of tiny
graves

that hold my past
miss taken
chances,

where I can walk
blindly
with my eyes facing the ground,

or roam
aimlessly
trying not to look back

at the corpsed
photo-frames
where regret is held within.

Looking

These things

keep getting worse,

I need to stop

seeing you everywhere.

In shopping centres,

in the faces of passers-by.

Driving on the opposite

side of the road.

In steamed up mirrors

when I need to wake up.

Late at night, beside me

when I'm lazy watching a film.

In unending dreams

of longed for happiness

punctuated by wishful

kisses

and bright sunlight

at 5am

that stirs me so

I wake up

looking for you next to me.

I got to stop

believing you'd be there.

Shell

As the dust settles in

to cracks

that were only drearily taped over,

the shell starts to look

a fraction of what it was

yet it is still flimsy

held together

but the tape won't last forever.

When the light of the world

shines on the weary shell,

it's clear the discolour

won't fade

after too long,

and all that's left

will simply wash away.

7-5-7

Alone, in a house for two
the other half is
left untarnished and quiet.
The hallway, the empty room
are kept but they lack
an idea. They collect dust.
The mono-painted white walls
have space where photos
don't hang, lacking memories.
The silence is near, it clings
to dusty curtains,
folds itself to windowsills.
In the living room darkness

hangs on in corners

and it perforates the gloom.

A space is left for nothing,

nothing doesn't come,

everything is left waiting.

All that we let escape

Our fingerprints dust

the glass of photo frames

of all the places we have left

behind

as if we were never really

there at all,

(it gets harder to recall)

and fragments of our silence

echo in the spaces

of all the places we were

before

like some kind of distant daydream

or misbegotten fairy-tale.

Our tread of footprints

indelible on the carpets

of places we once called

home,

now its harder to retrace

the feeling of being rooted,

grounded

somewhere we belong.

www.ingramcontent.com/pod-product-compliance
Lightning Source LLC
Chambersburg PA
CBHW051746130826
49812CB00033B/1019
* 9 7 8 9 3 5 7 2 1 3 4 0 0 *